PIANO | VOCAL | GUITAR

S0-AAA-617

TOP CHRISTIAN HITS
2014-2015

ISBN 978-1-4950-0572-5

HAL•LEONARD®
CORPORATION

7777 W. BLUEMOUND RD. P.O. BOX 13819 MILWAUKEE, WI 53213

Visit Hal Leonard Online at
www.halleonard.com

CONTENTS

DO SOMETHING

Words and Music by
MATTHEW WEST

Steady Pop beat

I woke up __ this morn - ing, __

saw a world full of trou - ble, now. __ I thought, "How'd we ev - er get so far down, and

The thought __ dis - gust - ed me, __ so I ___ shook my fist at heav - en. ___

I said, "God, why don't You do ___ some - thing?"

He said, "I did." Yeah. __ "I cre - at - ed

you."

live like __ an-gels __ of ap-a-thy who tell our-selves, __

"It's all right. Some-bod-y else -'ll do some-thing."

Well, I don't know a-bout __ you,

but I'm __ sick and __ ti-red of life with no de-si-re. I

FIX MY EYES

Words and Music by LUKE SMALLBONE,
JOEL SMALLBONE and SETH DAVID MOSLEY

THE GLORIOUS UNFOLDING

Words and Music by
STEVEN CURTIS CHAPMAN

With a solid beat

Lay __ your head down __ to-night, take a rest from __ the fight. __ Don't __ try to fig-ure it out, __ just

o-ver, so hold on ___ to ev-'ry prom - ise

God has made to us and watch _ this glo - ri - ous ___ un -

fold - ing. _____

God's plan from _ the start for this world and _ your heart has

GREATER

Words and Music by BART MILLARD,
MIKE SCHEUCHZER, NATHAN COCHRAN,
ROBBY SHAFFER, BARRY GRAUL,
DAVID GARCIA and BEN GLOVER

HE KNOWS MY NAME

Words and Music by MIA FIELDES,
FRANCESCA BATTISTELLI and SETH MOSLEY

Bright Pop feel

Spent to-day ___ in a con-ver-sa-tion in the mir-ror, face to face ___ with

some-bod-y less ___ than per-fect. I would-n't choose ___ me first ___ if

* Recorded a half step lower.

HOPE IN FRONT OF ME

Words and Music by DANNY GOKEY,
BERNIE HERMS and BRETT JAMES

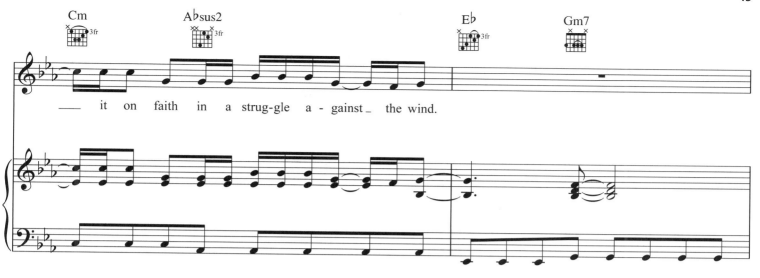

it on faith in a strug-gle a-gainst the wind.

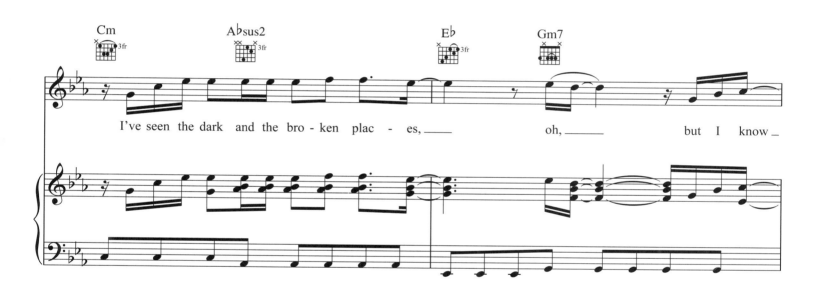

I've seen the dark and the bro-ken plac - es, oh, but I know

in my soul, no mat - ter how bad it gets, I'll be all

I AM

Words and Music by DAVID CROWDER
and ED CASH

Moderately

There's no space __ that His love can't reach. __ There's no place __ where we can't find peace. __ There's no end to a-maz-ing grace.

Take me in __ with Your

JESUS LOVES ME

Words and Music by REUBEN MORGAN,
CHRIS TOMLIN and BEN GLOVER

Lyrics:

I was lost, _____ I was in chains, _____ the world had a hold _____ of me. _____ My heart was a stone, _____ I was cov-ered in shame _____ when He came _____ for me.

It was a fire ___ deep in my soul. ___ I'll nev - er be ___

___ the same. ___ I stepped out of the dark ___ and in - to the light ___

when He called ___ my name. ___ I could - n't run, could - n't

run from His pres - ence. ___ I could - n't run, could - n't

MESSENGERS

Words and Music by LUKE SMALLBONE,
JOEL SMALLBONE, LE CRAE MOORE,
TORRANCE ESMOND, JOSEPH PRIELOZNY,
RICKY JACKSON, RANDY JACKSON
and KEN MACKEY

Pop Anthem feel

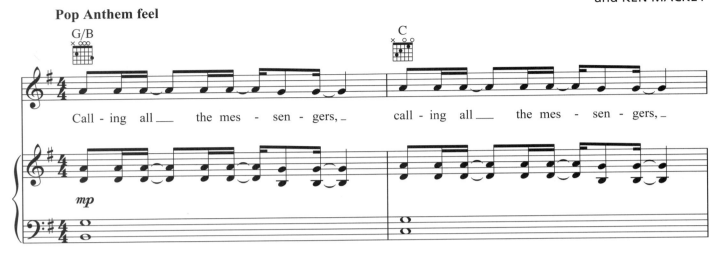

Additional Lyrics

2. I've been a lot of places where the scene ain't pretty.
I've seen plenty of hatred, death and destruction where ignorance kills many.
The blind leadin' the blind, we turnin' a blind eye.
That alone is a crime. We got the power to life.
I know that we make mistakes; don't let 'em keep you away.
Mercy, love and His grace is the reason we move ahead.
Speak out, though we never been qualified to do it.
I ain't earned it; I was loved into it. I'm brand-new, yeah.

MORE OF YOU

Words and Music by BEN GLOVER,
DAVID ARTHUR GARCIA and COLTON DIXON

MULTIPLIED

Words and Music by NATHANIEL "BO" RINEHART
and WILLIAM "BEAR" RINEHART

Folk Rock feel

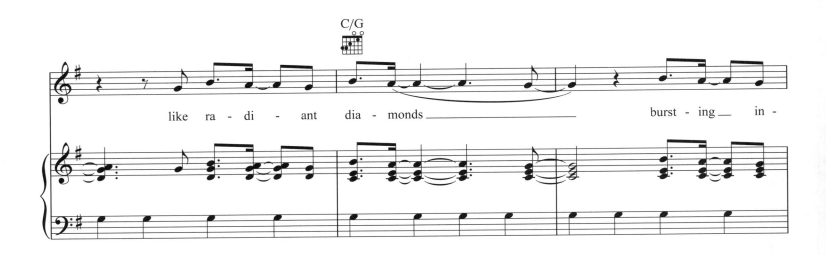

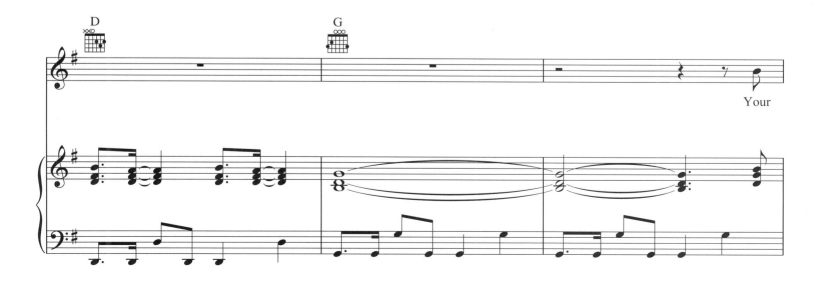

Your

MY HEART IS YOURS

Words and Music by JASON INGRAM,
KRISTIAN STANFILL, DANIEL CARSON
and BRETT YOUNKER

START A FIRE

Words and Music by CHAD MICHAEL MATTSON,
SETH DAVID MOSLEY and JONATHAN BURTON LOWRY

OCEANS
(Where Feet May Fail)

Words and Music by JOEL HOUSTON,
MATT CROCKER and SALOMON LIGHTHELM

Moderately slow

You call me out up-on the wa - ters, the great un - known where feet may ___ fail;

SHAKE

Words and Music by BEN GLOVER, DAVID GARCIA,
SOLOMON OLDS, BART MILLARD,
MIKE SCHEUCHZER, NATHAN COCHRAN,
ROBBY SHAFFER and BARRY GRAUL

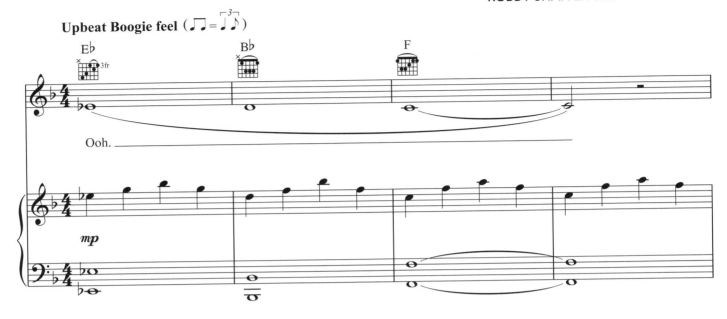

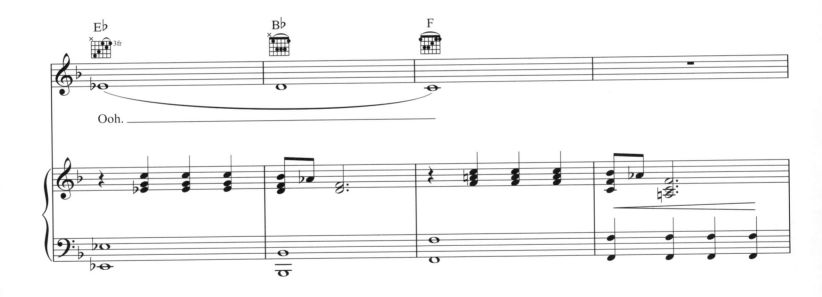

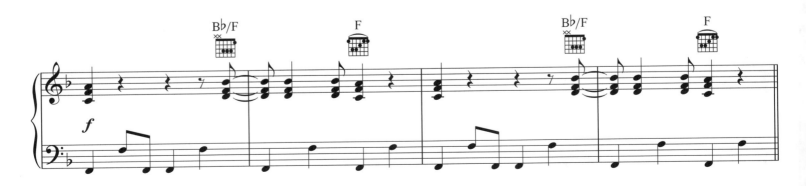

THIS IS AMAZING GRACE

Words and Music by PHIL WICKHAM,
JOSHUA NEIL FARRO and JEREMY RIDDLE

THRIVE

Words and Music by MARK HALL
and MATTHEW WEST

* *Recorded a half step lower.*

WATERFALL

Words and Music by CHRIS TOMLIN
and ED CASH

With energy

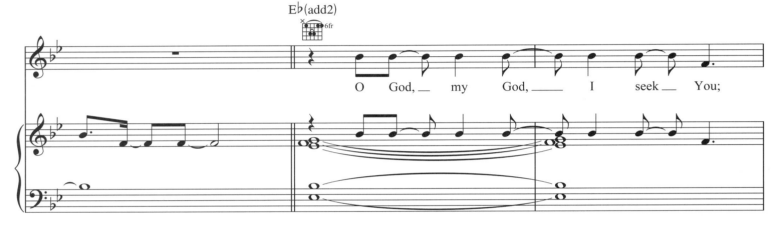

O God, — my God, — I seek — You;

I wan-na move when — You move. — You're more — than I —

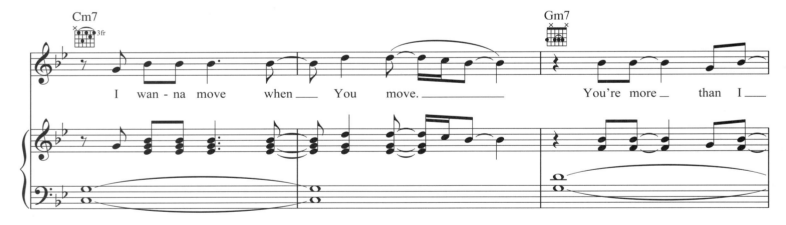

— could long — for; — I thirst for You. — You're an o-

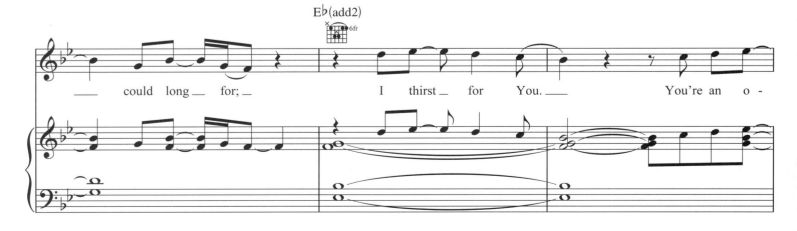

WE BELIEVE

Words and Music by TRAVIS RYAN,
MATTHEW HOOPER and RICHIE FIKE

WRITE YOUR STORY

Words and Music by BEN GLOVER
and FRANCESCA BATTISTELLI

Contemporary Christian Artist Folios from Hal Leonard
Arranged for Piano, Voice and Guitar

CASTING CROWNS – THRIVE
All the tracks from this popular Christian band's 2014 album, including the lead single "All You've Ever Wanted," plus: Broken Together • Dream for You • Follow Me • House of Their Dreams • Just Be Held • Thrive • and more.
00125333 P/V/G.............$16.99

THE JEREMY CAMP COLLECTION
A collection of 21 of this Dove Award-winner's best, including: Empty Me • Healing Hand of God • Jesus Saves • Let It Fade • Right Here • Stay • Take You Back • Walk by Faith • and more.
00307200 P/V/G.............$17.99

DAVID CROWDER*BAND – GIVE US REST
14 songs: After All (Holy) • Because He Lives • Come Find Me • Fall on Your Knees • I Am a Seed • Jesus, Lead Me to Your Healing Waters • Let Me Feel You Shine • Oh, Great Love of God • A Return • Sometimes • and more.
00307390 P/V/G.....................$16.99

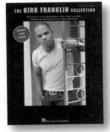

THE KIRK FRANKLIN COLLECTION
16 of Kirk Franklin's most popular gospel hits: Declaration (This Is It) • Help Me Believe • I Smile • Lean on Me • Looking for You • Jesus • Now Behold the Lamb • Stomp • Whatcha Lookin' 4? • Why We Sing • and more.
00307222 P/V/G.............$17.99

NATALIE GRANT – LOVE REVOLUTION
All 11 songs from the 2010 CD by this multi-Dove Award winner. Includes the hit single "Your Great Name" and: Beauty Mark • Daring to Be • Desert Song • The Greatness of Our God • Human • Love Revolution • Power of the Cross • Someday Our King Will Come • Song to the King • You Deserve.
00307164 P/V/G.....................$16.99

BRANDON HEATH – LEAVING EDEN
Matching folio to Dove Award-winning artist Brandon Heath's newest release. 11 tracks, including: As Long As I'm Here • It's Alright • It's No Good to Be Alone • The Light in Me • Might Just Save Your Life • Now More Than Ever • The One • Stolen • Your Love • and more.
00307208 P/V/G.....................$16.99

HILLSONG LIVE – GOD IS ABLE
11 songs from the 20th album by musicians and songwriters of Hillsong Church: Alive in Us • Cry of the Broken • The Difference • God Is Able • The Lost Are Found • My Heart Is Overwhelmed • Narrow Road • Rise • Unending Love • With Us • You Are More.
00307308 P/V/G.....................$16.99

KARI JOBE – WHERE I FIND YOU
12 songs from Jobe's sophomore CD: Find You on My Knees • Here • Love Came Down • One Desire • Rise • Run to You (I Need You) • Savior's Here • Stars in the Sky • Steady My Heart • We Are • We Exalt Your Name • What Love Is This.
00307381 P/V/G.....................$16.99

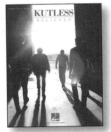

KUTLESS – BELIEVER
A baker's dozen from the chart-topping seventh CD from these Christian rockers. Contains the hit single "Carry Me to the Cross" and: All Yours • Believer • Carry On • Come Back Home • Even If • Identity • If It Ends Today • Need • This Is Love.
00307584 P/V/G.............$16.99

THE BEST OF MERCYME
20 of the best from these Texan Christian rockers, including: All of Creation • Beautiful • Bring the Rain • God with Us • Here with Me • Homesick • The Hurt and the Healer • I Can Only Imagine • Move • Word of God Speak • and more.
00118899 P/V/G.............$17.99

PASSION – LET THE FUTURE BEGIN
This matching songbook features the lead single "The Lord Our God," plus: Burning in My Soul • Children of Light • Come to the Water • In Christ Alone • Revelation Song • Shout • We Glorify Your Name • and more.
00119271 P/V/G.............$16.99

PHILLIPS, CRAIG & DEAN – THE ULTIMATE COLLECTION
31 songs spanning the career of this popular CCM trio: Favorite Song of All • Hallelujah (Your Love Is Amazing) • I Want to Be Just Like You • Shine on Us • Your Grace Still Amazes Me • and more.
00306789 P/V/G $19.95

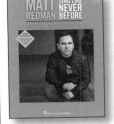

MATT REDMAN – SING LIKE NEVER BEFORE: THE ESSENTIAL COLLECTION
Our matching folio features 15 songs, including "10,000 Reasons (Bless the Lord)" and: Better Is One Day • The Father's Song • The Heart of Worship • Love So High • Nothing but the Blood • and more.
00116963 P/V/G.....................$16.99

THE SANCTUS REAL COLLECTION
14 songs: Alone • Closer • Don't Give Up • Everything About You • The Face of Love • Forgiven • I'm Not Alright • Lead Me • The Redeemer • Say It Loud • These Things Take Time • Turn On the Lights • We Need Each Other • Whatever You're Doing (Something Heavenly).
00307358 P/V/G.....................$16.99

SWITCHFOOT – THE BEST YET
This greatest hits compilation features the newly released song "This Is Home" and 17 other top songs. Includes: Concrete Girl • Dare You to Move • Learning to Breathe • Meant to Live • Only Hope • Stars • and more.
00307030 P/V/G $17.99

TENTH AVENUE NORTH – THE LIGHT MEETS THE DARK
The very latest from this Florida CCM band contains 11 songs, the hit single "You Are More" and: All the Pretty Things • Any Other Way • Empty My Hands • Healing Begins • House of Mirrors • Oh My Dear • On and On • Strong Enough to Save • The Truth Is Who You Are.
00307148 P/V/G.....................$16.99

THIRD DAY – MOVE
All 12 songs from the 2010 CD by these award-winning Christian rockers. Includes the hit single "Lift Up Your Face" and: Children of God • Everywhere You Go • Follow Me There • Gone • I'll Be Your Miracle • Make Your Move • Sound of Your Voice • Surrender • Trust in Jesus • What Have You Got to Lose.
00307186 P/V/G.....................$16.99

CHRIS TOMLIN – BURNING LIGHTS
A dozen songs from the 2013 release from this Christian songwriting giant! Includes the lead single "Whom Shall I Fear (God of Angel Armies)" plus: Awake My Soul • Countless Wonders • God's Great Dance Floor • Lay Me Down • Sovereign • and more.
00115644 P/V/G.....................$16.99

0514